LIFE IS A JOURNEY,
NOT A DESTINATION

LIFE IS A JOURNEY, NOT A DESTINATION

Simple Ways to Find Peace, Joy, and Happiness in Your Everyday Life

T. C. DOWNING

Printed in the United States of America.

ISBN: 978-1-4669-1265-6 (sc)
ISBN: 978-1-4669-1267-0 (hc)
ISBN: 978-1-4669-1266-3 (e)

Library of Congress Control Number: 2012901139

Trafford rev. 03/08/2012

 www.trafford.com

North America & international
toll-free: 1 888 232 4444 (USA & Canada)
phone: 250 383 6864 ♦ fax: 812 355 4082

CONTENTS

This book is dedicated to Lorne.
Your wonderful spirit and wisdom
will always live on in my heart.

ACKNOWLEDGMENTS

To my parents, you showered me with unconditional love, and showed me my worth as a human being. You let me make my mistakes and learn from them without saying "I told you so." Thank you for all the quality time you spent with me, I learned from an early age that I was important and what I said mattered. You created the solid foundation that I have built my life upon—for this I will be forever grateful. There is not a day that goes by that I don't thank God for having such awesome parents. You are both amazing role models!

To my husband, you are my rock. I love you with all my heart. Thank you for twenty wonderful years of marriage. I couldn't have imagined anyone else by my side! You bring fun and laughter to my life. Don't ever change, your love of life is infectious, and brings joy to all those around you!

To Nathan and Samantha, you are my gifts from God. You bring absolute joy to my life! Because of you, I have evolved as a person and experienced depths of emotion that I hadn't thought possible. I hope dad and I have given you the tools to live a happy and joyous life, and that you remember; life is a journey, not a destination!

INTRODUCTION

Life Is a Journey, Not a Destination, will teach, inspire, and coach you to discover peace, joy, and happiness in your everyday life. With the combination of stories and practical action steps, you will be guided to—discover who you really are—forgive your past mistakes—reconnect with your spouse—be present with your kids.

I will share with you what more than twenty years of research and working in the service industry have helped me achieve. The stories from my clients have helped improve my knowledge, and I have observed over and over again that people are always searching for answers—How can I be a better parent?—How do I deal with the stresses in my everyday life?

Read this book as a light hearted "advice" book from someone who has noticed that, when I have shared what has worked for me, others have become inspired to do the same, resulting in positive changes ... ENJOY!

Chapter One

WHO ARE YOU?

To EMBARK ON the journey of life, it's important to know yourself. When you know who you are, you create your life according to *you*. Too often people are living their lives according to an identity that someone else has created for them. Are you living a life full of joy and happiness? Are you unknowingly creating a life that you are unhappy with, because you have lost touch with who you are?

What brings you joy? Take a moment to really think about the last time you felt truly joyous and happy. What if I told you that you could experience these emotions more often? You can, but first you need to get in touch with the person that is you.

Are you your authentic self? Are you in denial about who you are? Are you wearing a social mask with family, friends or co-workers? Have you made mistakes in the past that you are not proud of? Are you living a lie? These are all things that will prevent you from living your best life if you don't get honest with yourself, and others. If you are pretending to be something you are not, you will never become all that you can be.

Be your *true self*. You are not perfect. No one is. If you have made mistakes, forgive yourself and accept that you did your best with what you knew in the moment. Know that everything you do in life, including your mistakes can show you how to change your life for the better. Learn to love yourself from where you are right now in your life. Be the best you can be, but at the same time, free yourself from trying to be perfect.

You are the foundation that you build your life upon. Make your foundation strong; find out *who you really are*. Remember that living a wonderful happy life starts from within, it starts with you!

EXERCISE

1. Who are you? What are your greatest qualities? Think about all the great things that make you who you are.

2. What are your interests? What are you passionate about?

3. Take time for yourself. You deserve it. Think of something that you can spend at least a half an hour a day doing that is just for you. This is your time. Do not feel guilty. Just remember, when you take better care of yourself you can take better care of others.

4. Make a list of at least five things that you love to do.

5. Do them. Try to do at least one a week. You will notice the more you do things that

bring you joy; the more joyous things will start showing up in your life.

6. Are there aspects of yourself that you try to hide, due to fear of rejection or being judged? You will not live the life of your dreams if you are somehow denying who you really are. Be your authentic self.

7. Are you living a lie? How would your life improve if you lived your truth? Would a burden be lifted? If so, free yourself!

Chapter Two

OPPOSITES ATTRACT

HARMONIOUS RELATIONSHIPS BETWEEN men and women can be challenging. Problems arise when we expect or assume the opposite sex should feel, think, or act the way we do. We often feel like we live in different realities because of our lack of knowledge, mutual experiences, and understanding of how we both communicate.

When I had a problem I just wanted my husband to listen—he just wanted to solve it. When there was something bothering him, I tried to help him by discussing it—he just wanted to handle the problem himself before he opened up about it. This drove us crazy until we accepted that we just didn't communicate in the same way. He eventually learned that when I have a problem he should just let me talk, and I, to give him his space until he is ready to discuss it. This has saved us from many arguments and hurt feelings. It has made me realize the secret to having a harmonious relationship is mainly about *realizing the differences between men and women.*

Times have changed; we no longer share the same gender roles of our ancestors. Deep down we all have our instinctive human desire to feel like a man or a woman. We just need to understand and adjust them to the way we live today. It is just a matter of *knowing our differences* that enables us to be more understanding of the opposite sex.

Women are natural nurturers. They love to take care of others; it's how they show their love. Often a woman is most happy when she can take care of the people around her. Some challenges facing women today are the difficulties of juggling home, work, and family. It leaves them feeling overwhelmed. This can add major stress to a woman's life.

As a woman you need to be aware when you are giving too much. It is fine to take care of those you love, but not to the point of feeling angry and resentful towards them—*you need to know your limits.*

Men often feel that they need to be self-reliant. They are often focussed on providing for their loved ones and bury their own emotions. In today's stressful world, and fast pace, this may lead to emotions becoming bottled up and reaching a boiling point—to help prevent this men need to get in touch with their emotions.

It's also instinctive for men to want to provide for those they love. In the past men were the providers for their families. Now it may take both the man and the woman working to support a household. This is just a reflection of modern times and not a reflection of their ability to provide.

What does a woman want in a relationship? A woman wants to feel like a woman. She wants a man who is confident and who can handle a situation calmly, without being controlling. If a woman knows that the man can handle the situation, she won't feel the need to control it. A woman wants to feel protected and cherished. She wants fidelity, and commitment. She wants a man to see if she is struggling, and help her. She wants a man who listens, and is her biggest supporter. She wants to give up the control, without being controlled.

What does a man want in a relationship? Men need to be needed and wanted by their partners. A man wants love, fidelity and commitment. He doesn't want to be a mind reader, if he asks you what is wrong, he wants the truth. Men want a manipulative free relationship. They want a partner who communicates without being critical. They want a woman who is emotionally stable. Men just want to make their partners happy. They are most satisfied when their partners are happy!

To make a relationship work it's important to embrace our differences. Learn to love and appreciate each other for who we are.

If there are problems, try to work on them from a realistic standpoint. No one is perfect, *including you*. Get back to the reasons why you fell in love and chose this person in the first place.

You need to invest time when it comes to your relationship. It's like your bank account; you can't keep making withdrawals if you haven't made any recent deposits. If you don't take the time to nurture your relationship, you may wake up one morning and realize you have fallen out of love with that person. Those feelings of disconnection may lead to an attraction to someone else. Often affairs happen not because of the sex, but how that other person makes them feel emotionally. Even if you leave, start over with someone else, and don't nurture the relationship, chances are you will find yourself in the same situation in the future. Why put yourself through all that. Fall back in love with the person you fell in love with!

EXERCISE

1. Make a list of the great qualities your partner has.

2. How has your life been enriched because of your partner?

3. What attracted you to your partner in the beginning?

4. What can you do to let your partner know that you love and appreciate him/her?

5. If you have been arguing lately, sit down calmly, without blame and see if there is a way to relieve the situation.

6. Organize date nights. If you feel like you have lost touch with your partner, get to know each other again. Get back to the feelings of togetherness that were there in the beginning.

Chapter Three

YOUR KIDS, ARE THEY WORTHY OF YOUR LOVE? DO THEY KNOW IT? ARE YOU SURE?

KIDS DON'T NEED the latest gadgets or the exotic vacations. They need *you*! They need to know that they are special enough that you *want* to spend time with them. Not only do they need your presence, they need you to *be present*! When you are with them they need to know that they are seen and heard. This shows them their value and worth as a human being.

When I was growing up my parents often made *ordinary outings extraordinary*. When we would go cross country skiing we would pack a thermos of hot chocolate and a lunch, stop along the way and have our "winter picnic."

We lived near the ocean and went often but they still managed to make the excursions fun with treasure hunts and roasting hot dogs and marshmallows.

If we were stuck in the house on a rainy afternoon we would play board games, the winners getting to choose from a bowl of surprises kept in the cupboard especially for those occasions.

These are all things that didn't cost much and took very little effort, but it made us *feel special*. It was quality time, and as an adult I look back on all those times with fond memories.

One night when my kids were young, we put their snowsuits over their pyjamas and went outside in the backyard to play with them in the snow. They were so thrilled to be outside past their bedtime, plus the fact that we were outside making snow angels right along with them, added to their excitement. This today is one of their most cherished childhood memories.

When your kids get older and look back on their lives, they won't always remember what you bought them, *but they will definitely remember the quality time spent together.* By doing special things with your kids, no matter what their age, you are providing them with wonderful memories that they will treasure and maybe one day do with their own children.

EXERCISE

---

1. Take an activity that you have done in the past together and make it an event. Add special things to make it different. Be totally present with them when you do the activity. Be aware of how this time is different than the time before. You will probably notice the simplest gestures will result in the greatest pleasures.

2. Do your kids have the "I have therefore I am" syndrome? Are they validating their self worth by the *stuff* they own? If so how can you shift this?

3. Do you assume that your kids know you love them and that you enjoy spending time with them? Make it a point to let them know.

4. Do you often come home tired and notice what your children haven't done? Can you find things they did do well and let them know?

5. Every year on their birthday write them a letter about how they have enriched your life in the past year. Be specific. Keep them in a safe place. These are irreplaceable and will give them much joy in the years to come.

Chapter Four

YOUR HOME-YOUR SOFT CLOUD

I HAVE ALWAYS considered my home to be my soft cloud; a place where my family can come to at the end of a tiring day and cushions us from the bumps of life. We know here we will be surrounded by comfort and love. It's a place where we make the effort to keep it stress free. If there is tension, we try to work it out, get to the root of the problem and try to prevent it from reoccurring in the future. Our home is filled with love, not only for each other, but also for the friends we welcome in.

I can't stress enough how important it is to try to limit the amount of stress and negativity that exists in your home. Whether you live alone, with a partner, or with kids, you are all responsible for creating and maintaining a peaceful environment. If your home is not as you would like it. Change it. Sit down with everyone and work out what is bringing negative energy into your home. Really look at it from all points of view and try to be accepting of other people's faults and differences.

If your home is cluttered, clean it out and get rid of what you don't need. If you're surrounded by too much stuff, donate it.

If there are home projects to be done, stop stressing over it. Make a list of all the projects and prioritize them. Commit to doing them and write a reasonable time line for each one to get them done. This takes them out of your head, eliminates the mental clutter and permits you to break them down into feasible tasks. Try to find ways you can do them and even have fun in the process. Involve your partner and your kids. Make it quality time spent together and you can all bask in the feeling of accomplishment that executing a plan from start to finish brings you. Once you do this a few times and are able to cross them off the list you will want to tackle the other ones.

If your home is constantly busy and hurried, try to slow it down. Turn off the television, turn down the lights, play some soft music, and the rhythm of your home will eventually follow. If the energy in your home is gloomy, watch some funny movies, or play joyful music—incorporate more activities that bring fun and laughter to all who live there.

EXERCISE

1. Think of three reoccurring problems that cause stress or negativity in your home.

2. What can you and your family do to work through these issues and prevent them in the future. Get everyone on board to help come up with solutions.

3. Are you inviting people or situations into your home that create negativity? If so, how can you resolve this?

Chapter Five

FIGHT OR FLIGHT

IMAGINE YOU'RE A caveman, you duck into a cave to seek shelter from the rain and you come face to face with a saber-tooth tiger. Your body immediately goes in the "fight or flight" mode. Your heart beats two or three times faster, adrenaline pumps through your body giving you strength, tiny blood vessels shut down, your pupils dilate, and you can jump higher and run faster than you could have ever imagined. You luckily escape due to your supercharged body, and you live to see another day.

Back in the caveman days "fight or flight" was important for survival. An encounter with a saber-tooth tiger was life or death—not so anymore. Our present day "saber-tooth tigers" are rush hour traffic, job dissatisfaction, arguments with your spouse, or financial problems. What was originally the body's tool to help you survive a life or death situation, has now become mainly false alarms or *chronic stress*.

Chronic stress disrupts nearly every system in the body. It has been attributed to such things as high blood pressure, heart attack and stroke, infertility, and premature aging. Not only does chronic stress effect us physically it also effects us emotionally.

When our "fight or flight" system is activated, we tend to perceive everything in our environment as a possible threat to our survival. Our brain switches to "attack mode," this causes us to perceive almost everything in our world as a possible threat. We narrow our focus to those things that can harm us. We see everything through the filter of fear and danger.

What we don't see is the joy and happiness in our lives. We soon become oblivious to the wonderful things around us. Our consciousness is focused on fear, not love and joy.

Long term stress can rewire our brains, leaving us susceptible to anxiety and depression. We lose the ability to notice and appreciate all the wonderful things to be grateful for.

Often in today's fast paced life, chronic stress has become so familiar, it is almost *normal*.

The good news is we all have the power to change the amount of stress we experience in our lives! You might not always be able to avoid stressful situations, but you can control the way you respond to them. Managing stress is all about taking charge of your life. By being aware of your thoughts, your emotions, your schedules, and your relationships, you can make the necessary changes to reduce the amount of stress you experience in your day to day life.

You need to decide if the stressful situations you are constantly experiencing are worth the physical and mental side effects. You need to ask yourself "does this situation really warrant triggering my "fight or flight" survival mode? Is this really a saber—tooth tiger?"

EXERCISE

1. Are you constantly in a state of "fight or flight?" If so, go through the areas of your life where you find yourself stressed, and think of ways that being pro-active may help eliminate these stressful situations. For example, if being stuck in traffic stresses you because you might be late for work, make it a habit to leave earlier. If you are trying to have a home cooked meal on the table every night, and often because of traffic, have to order takeout, perhaps spend a day off work, cooking and freezing meals that you can use during the week.

2. For those stressful situations that you cannot prevent by being pro-active, then you must change how you feel about the situation and how you react to it. Think of ways that you can eliminate or diminish the effects these

situations have on you emotionally. Maybe ask yourself the question "will this matter a year from now?" If the answer is "no" then it shouldn't matter now!

Chapter Six

WHAT GOES AROUND COMES AROUND, NEWTON'S THIRD PHYSICAL LAW OF MOTION

NEWTON CHANGED OUR understanding of the universe with his three laws of motion. The third law of motion being, for every force there is a reaction force that is equal in size, but opposite in direction. For every action there is a reaction, or in other words *what goes around comes around!*

Do you live your life by this law? Do you knowingly by word or action, cause others hurt or pain? Do you treat others as you would like to be treated?

If you want to know how you have used Newton's third law of motion in your life, look around you. Your life is a mirror, it reflects back to you who you are. Are you surrounded by loving people? If so, you have been loving. Are you surrounded by negative people? Then you have been negative or have let negative people influence you.

Whatever you send out you are getting back—always keep this in mind as you go through your day. If you spend an hour gossiping and trashing someone, you are inviting the same back. When someone makes you angry and you spend time and energy on revenge, you are inviting the same back in your life. If you spend time being kind and loving, guess what you are going to receive? Love and kindness! Now which would you prefer?

Whatever you would like to have more of in your life, learn to give it first. You want love, give love. You want respect, give respect. You want money, give money. You want to be successful, help someone become successful.

What goes around comes around. Spend time in gratitude, and you will attract back to you things to be grateful for!

EXERCISE

1. The energy you generate designs your life. What life are you currently designing for yourself?

2. Do you have friends in your life who are constant sources of negativity? How can you prevent this? Maybe it's time to redefine your friendships, the subjects you talk about, or form new friendships with more positive people.

3. Are there situations in your life that are bringing back bad energy to you? What can you do to change them?

4. Think of something you would like to have more of in your life and as you go through your day give it to others. Notice how it comes back to you in other ways.

Chapter Seven

COLLECT MEMORIES, NOT THINGS

TAKE THE TIME to do things with the special people in your life. Spend quality time with them and capture it through photos. Put them in frames and place them in areas where you will see them and appreciate the great moments and awesome people you have in your life.

I sometimes drive my husband and kids crazy with my need to take pictures that tell a story of our outings or family vacations. I didn't do this every outing, but certainly for every vacation, no matter how big or small. When we look through the albums, we relive those wonderful moments.

I remember when my son was little he loved Winnie The Pooh, so one day we went to the park and pretended we were in the Hundred acre Wood. We climbed over logs, walked along paths, calling for Tigger and Eeyore. We had an amazing time. When I look back at those pictures I'm brought back to that day.

It's the little moments and the people in your life that make life special. Go through life creating and collecting memories and surround yourself with reminders. It can either be pictures or little souvenirs, maybe a pebble from the river, a shell from the ocean, or a leaf from the forest. Put them somewhere where you will be continuously reminded of the awesome life you have. Feel blessed to have each other.

One year for Christmas I gave my husband a picture frame filled with pictures of just the two of us on our many little adventures. When I was finished I couldn't believe all the things we had done together. I remember looking at the frame feeling so grateful to have him in my life and to have been so blessed to have done so many things together. It now hangs in his office and when he is having a rough day he looks at the pictures and it reminds him how blessed he is. Now we look for more adventures and things to do together so that we can fill up another frame.

In placing our pictures and souvenirs all around our home, I'm constantly reminded of our wonderful life. The simple act of putting my morning coffee on my table beside one of my pictures brings a smile to my face. Placing my keys on the entrance table beside a sea shell I collected from a scuba diving trip with my son makes me feel so blessed. By placing souvenirs all around my home I am continuously reminded of what is important in my life and any minor upsets just melt away.

Although it is very important to live in the present, still appreciate the past and dream about the future!

EXERCISE

1. Think about times in the past that brought you joy. Put pictures or items that remind you of those times and place them where you will see them often.

Chapter Eight

ARE YOU A JACK OF ALL TRADES, MASTER OF NONE?

WHEN YOU HAVE kids you go through an identity shift. One day you are focused on your career, the next day, being a parent. How do you manage both, and do it well?

Even though you can be amazing at both, pick one that you will excel at and let that be your priority. If I would have been given this advice it would have saved me much guilt and self doubt. You see, I tried to excel at both, and although at times possible, but not always sustainable. I thought that I had to be master at both and constantly struggled to do just that. When I didn't see the results I was expecting at work, I blamed myself. Thought I wasn't good enough, smart enough, and ambitious enough.

When I was at work I was thinking of home, when I was at home I was thinking of work. When one of my kids was sick and I had to take a day off, I felt horrible. I felt like I was unreliable. Then because of the guilt and pressure of not being at work, I often found it hard to concentrate on taking care of my sick child!

It was a vicious circle. I thought that if I just worked harder I would finally master both. I always had this feeling of wanting to do better in my career, and it seemed the minute I started to advance, circumstance arose where I would have to focus on my family. Of course, my family would come first, and often times at the expense of my career. Don't get me wrong, I absolutely love my family, they are my life. I don't regret one moment of having to put aside my career for them, I would do it all again in a heartbeat.

What I wouldn't do again is put myself through the guilt and feelings of inadequacy. I would get clear on the fact that, it is what it is. I'm not a superwoman. I would know that for a few years I would only master one area and that would be my family. It was very difficult seeing other people at work advancing ahead of me and thinking it was about my skill or how I did my job. Now when I look back, most of those other people weren't in the "I just had kids phase of their lives," so it was understandable that they advanced further than I did at that time.

But because I wasn't clear in my own mind, I felt like a jack of all trades, master of none!

EXERCISE

1. Are you currently struggling with trying to excel at both career and family? If so, what can you do to ease the struggle?

Chapter Nine

AND THE CAT CAME BACK
THE VERY NEXT DAY . . .

SO HERE YOU are, in your happy place. You surround yourself with positive loving people. You feel like you are in a great place. You have banished negativity. Then you go to work, and you dislike your boss, a supervisor or a co-worker. You have to be exposed to this person daily.

In your personal life you can choose who you surround yourself with but not so at work. You have to ask yourself "Can I change this person?" No. "Can I change the energy I bring when I'm in contact with them?" Yes.

If you find that you are exposed to someone daily whom you don't like or you have had a rocky start, try to write down or think of something positive about that person. Don't lie to yourself but I'm sure if you think hard enough you can find at least one good quality. Start from there.

Once you are able to create some positive thoughts about that person, try to think those thoughts when you are in their presence. If the opportunity presents itself, try to verbally compliment them on those qualities. It will really change the energy surrounding both of you.

I have used this technique many times, and have noticed that with just my thoughts I was able to change the energy surrounding us both. Strange but true! I now have great relationships with people whom I got off to a rocky start with by using this method. Often it is just a misunderstanding or misconception about that person. Thoughts are things; use them to turn situations around.

EXERCISE

1. Is there someone in your daily life that you don't like for whatever reason, but have no choice but to be exposed to, or work with them? Can you think of at least one good quality about them? The next time you are together, think about that quality, or better yet compliment them on it. Watch the energy between you both shift. Make sure you are honest and authentic when you do this. You may never fully like this person, but by concentrating on that one good quality you may discover more!

Chapter Ten

LIVE IN GRATITUDE

SOMETIMES WE ARE so busy living or striving for the things we want, we forget to be grateful for the things we already do have! We go through our daily lives thinking we will be happy only when we have reached the next level in our lives, when we get that promotion, or when we get that new house. Life is too short not to appreciate every day.

It is sad that it usually takes hearing about something tragic for us to look at our lives and be grateful for who or what we have. We suddenly gain perspective on our own lives and think we are not going to sweat the small stuff. This usually lasts until the next "small" thing arrives and we are back to sweating it! We need to be appreciative and grateful as we go through our daily lives for the gifts we receive each day, no matter how small.

"I cried because I had no shoes until I met a man with no feet."
—Persian proverb

We need to know that no matter how tough we have it, there are people out there who have it worse. There are people in the world right now who are burying a loved one, a mother, a father, or a child. There are people out there who have had their whole families wiped out by genocide. There are kids who are right now losing limbs to land mines. Even if you are experiencing tough times in your life, try to find things that you can be grateful for.

When we live in gratitude we will bring more things in our lives to be grateful for. Even if you live in the smallest apartment with the most threadbare furnishings, be grateful for what you do have. I'm not saying, to one day not want for something better, by all means-dream big! Just be grateful for what you have in the moment.

EXERCISE

1. What are the things you are most grateful for in your life?

2. Every morning before you get out of bed, feel the gratitude for all the wonderful things in your life.

Chapter Eleven

DON'T ENTER A PISSING CONTEST WITH A SKUNK, BECAUSE YOU JUST CAN'T WIN

MY DAD ALWAYS told me not to do things to make people talk. Living in a small town, this can be difficult. Nonetheless, most of my earlier years I tried to live by this rule. After I was married there was a rumour that was being circulated by a family member about me. It was mean spirited and completely false. In the past this family member had caused many problems in the family with her vicious tongue as well as for other people in the community. I was talking to a dear man who used to be my principal in high school. I really valued his opinion and was telling him that I was thinking of going to confront this family member, to stop these rumours that she was spreading. I was bemoaning the fact that even though I didn't do anything to make people talk, they were anyway. It wasn't fair.

He calmly listened to my dilemma and then said "Don't enter a pissing contest with a skunk, because you just can't win." He went on to explain, "by this I mean that if you stop this rumour there will be many more from where that one came from. This is her specialty; this is what she is good at. She is a skunk, and anyone who ever enters a pissing contest with a skunk, just can't win! Let it go."

This went against everything I believed in. "This is my good name and reputation we are talking about. I have to defend it! Nip this in the bud. What are people going to think if I don't stop these rumours?" I asked. "The people, who really *know* you, won't believe it, and if the rest don't know you well enough, then why care? Eventually she will work her way down the line and the people who were so quick to believe it, will fall victim to her vicious tongue. Accept it, she is a skunk. Don't waste anymore energy on it as you can't control other people and what they say. No matter how hard you try to live your life so people won't talk, if that is who they are, they will talk anyway. They are skunks!"

This transformed my life. I no longer live my life worrying what someone might say about me, because as we all know, there are a lot of skunks out there!

EXERCISE

1. Can you think of a time when you entered a pissing contest with a skunk and didn't win?

2. Have you ever been or are you currently being exposed to "skunks" in your life?

3. Could you, in the future, see them for what they are "skunks" and let it go?

Chapter Twelve

STUPID PEOPLE SYNDROME-SPS

UNLESS YOU LIVE under a rock you will most probably have to put up with stupid people affecting the mood you are in. One minute you are thanking the universe, God, the higher power or whatever you wish to call it, for all your wonderful blessings when WHAM some stupid person cuts you off in traffic. Since I don't like how the word stupid resonates within me, I tell myself they are suffering from a disease called stupid people syndrome or SPS for short. This way I don't have to say the word stupid, and it gives me hope that although they might suffer from that syndrome now, maybe in the future, they will find a cure!

So how to deal with people who suffer from SPS? Well since each situation is different and often comes when you are least expecting it, just try to not let it affect you emotionally. Remember you can only control yourself, so try to put the situation in perspective. Don't rehash it or over think it. Feel whatever emotions are fitting, and then quickly let them go and move on. Just accept that there are people out there who suffer from SPS. That's it, that's all. Learn to live with them.

Maybe in the future take it as a challenge in mastering your emotions and see how quickly you can get over it. Better yet, turn it into a funny scenario in your head where you see the person laying on a psychiatrists' couch, getting help for their SPS. Do whatever it takes to get back to that great mood you were in before your paths crossed.

EXERCISE

1. Start noticing where your great mood is altered by people suffering from SPS. Think of ways you can minimize the effects that people suffering from SPS have in your life. Look for patterns. Does it happen most when you are driving? Maybe play calming music and place a lavender scented air freshener in your car to help keep you in a calm state while driving.

2. Do not waste time trying to figure out the "why" of the situation. This will just have you wracking your brains trying to understand them from your perspective. Since you don't suffer from SPS you will probably never know why people who suffer from it, do what they do. Try to come up

with scenarios or tools you could use to get you out of that negative state as quickly as possible and maybe even put some humour in the situation. Be creative!

Chapter Thirteen

MAJOR IN THE MINORS

WE OFTEN FIND ourselves getting caught up in trivial things. A co-worker says something hurtful, you feel someone let you down, or a stranger is inconsiderate. These are minor things but in the moment cause major negative emotions. It's ok to feel the hurt, resentment, frustration, anger, or whatever emotion the situation brings to you. Feel it, put it in perspective and move on. Remember that, like attracts like and the longer you harbour those negative emotions the more you attract those negative emotions to you.

A co worker was thanking me for having helped her with a problem. She wanted to offer me a thank you present for having been so nice, and was asking me what I would like. I told her it was my pleasure, and jokingly said that "I was always nice so why did this time warrant a gift?" Another co worker who was listening to our exchange said scowling "no, you are not always nice." I immediately went from feeling good for having helped someone, to being insulted.

I have never been mean to this girl; in fact the contrary. Then I thought "what if she did feel like I had been mean to her?" Her proper course of action could have been to come see me to discuss the problem instead of intruding in on a conversation with a snarky remark. For at least ten minutes the comment went around in my mind and the unfairness of it upset me.

That's when I decided that from then on when my great emotions were changed by someone or something for negative ones, I was going to turn it around. I decided that when that happened I was going to text something nice to someone I cared about, my husband, my kids, or a friend. So that is exactly what I did. I texted my friend "you're awesome". She responded back with a beautiful text, and now I was back to feeling great. Even when someone is being insensitive or mean you can always think of someone who you love and appreciate. So that is what I do now. It totally changes my mood.

EXERCISE

1. Imagine ways that you can change negative emotions in minor situations, to feeling great in a major way.

Chapter Fourteen

IT JUST MAKES SENSE TO USE YOUR SENSES

THE QUICKEST WAY to change your emotions is through your senses. Have you ever been in a great mood and something you see, hear, touch, smell, or taste, upset you? Our senses are very powerful and have an immediate effect on our emotions.

Many years ago I worked for a boss who was very controlling and any interaction with him always left me doubting my self-worth. There was a coffee shop across the hall and the smell of hazelnut coffee often wafted over. After five years I quit working there, but the smell of hazelnut coffee always sent me right back to those feelings of worthlessness.

When I was pregnant, for the first three months, I experienced mind numbing exhaustion. A year after giving birth, I started using a perfume that I hadn't used since those first few months of pregnancy. As soon as I would put it on, my body felt physically exhausted. After a week I stopped using it and I immediately felt better. I hadn't realized it, but my brain had linked that smell with the feeling of exhaustion and it just put me back in that tired state.

These are all examples of aromas, but have you ever had a sad moment in your life, maybe the breakup of a relationship and there is a certain song playing in the background? Years later, when you hear that song, you are brought back to that feeling of sadness and heartbreak.

Let's look at the flip side. Have you ever had a wonderful vacation, and months late use coconut scented hand soap, which reminded you of your suntan lotion? You can practically feel the sun on your face and hear the ocean. Did your Grandmother make bread when you were a kid, and the smell of yeast or bread baking can immediately take you back to those feelings of being cherished and loved? Noticing how my senses so vividly recreated an experience or emotions in my life, I tried a little experiment.

My husband and I were feeling tired, stressed and disconnected from each other. We booked a lovely romantic getaway for two nights, which included a suite with a Jacuzzi, a fireplace and a spa package for treatments and massages. Before leaving, I purchased a line of products including a room spray, soap, bath salts and candles-all in the same scent. We basically stayed in our robes for two days, and if we weren't at the spa doing our treatments, we were curled in front of the fireplace or in the Jacuzzi. Because of the bath salts, candles, and room spray, it became our theme scent for relaxation, well being, and feeling connected to each other.

Afterwards whenever we were feeling stressed or disconnected, I would prepare a bath, spray the room scent and light the candles that we had used for our spa getaway. Time just slipped away and it was like we were back there, feeling the feelings of well being and connection. It was instantaneous and worked like a charm. I realized that by putting my senses to work for me it, I was creating more positive feelings and emotions in my life.

So get your senses working for you; after all, it just makes sense to use your senses!

EXERCISE

1. Decide what feelings or emotions you would like to experience more of in your life. Choose which one of your senses you would like to use to eventually recreate those emotions. It can be a scent, a picture, or even a song.

2. Do whatever it takes to get into that emotional state you would like to recreate in the future. Once you are powerfully feeling those emotions, use one of the five senses that you have chosen. If it's a scent, spray it, if it's a song, have it play while you are experiencing those emotions or that experience. Do this repeatedly until you are sure you have connected those emotions with your sensory triggers

3. As you go through your day use the triggers you have chosen to experience those wonderful feelings.

Chapter Fifteen

Anger is like nitrous oxide

IF YOU ARE striving to live your best life does anger fit anywhere into the equation? I had lost a considerable amount of money to which I felt were shady business partners. I had a hard time even getting myself out of bed in the morning. I was in a dark place. For years I had put in a lot of hours to make the venture work. I had sacrificed time spent away from my family and invested a large sum of money. I couldn't get past the fact that it wasn't fair.

I felt powerless and desperate. I needed to find better emotions to get myself through these hard times. I wanted so much to feel happiness and joy but couldn't due to my current feelings of helplessness and despair. So I let the anger kick in about the situation. It gave me the strength I needed to pull myself out of the dark hole I was in. My anger—which in the past didn't always serve me well—helped me to overcome my feelings of despair.

So yes, I think anger can have its resources but a word of caution, use it sparingly. I like to think of it as nitrous oxide. Race car drivers use it to give them bursts of speed and power during a race, but if they use it too much or too often, it will destroy their engine. So use it to give you strength, but once it has served its purpose, let it go, because too much of it, like the nitrous oxide, it will destroy your chance of winning in life.

EXERCISE

1. Are you experiencing too much anger in your life? If so decide if it is serving you or if it is holding you back.

2. What changes can you make in your life today to let go of the anger that does not serve you?

3. Is there an area in your life right now where anger could give you the strength to overcome a situation and help you reach for the better emotions in life?

Chapter Sixteen

JUST BECAUSE WE BREAK, DOES THAT MEAN WE ARE BROKEN?

MOST OFTEN IT is only through the bad times that we grow. Why is that? Shouldn't we be looking at the joy we experience in life and be asking ourselves "how can I get myself more of that?" You would think so, after all, we are intelligent human beings! But alas, no, that is not the way it works. Often we have to break first. But just because we break, does that mean we are broken?

When I was suing my business partners, I felt helpless. Most times in court cases, whoever has the most money wins. By this time I had none. I was in a situation where I couldn't afford to lose the money and couldn't afford to sue for it either. I naively thought they couldn't get away with this. There wouldn't be a judge in the world that wouldn't make them return my money. So I sued. I felt like David versus Goliath! I felt powerless.

I remember coming home one day to a stack of bills in my mailbox. I carried them upstairs opening them along the way. There were three cancelation notices; my electricity, cable service, and my home phone—all due to unpaid bills. I couldn't pay them! I couldn't pay the mortgage! I couldn't even buy groceries. I had lost all our money. What had I done to our family? I had worked so hard to better our lives, and instead was faced with losing our home. I couldn't see a way out. I broke down. I walked over to a patch of sun coming in through my patio door, sank down to the floor and sobbed uncontrollably for hours.

Eventually I stood up—it wasn't easy-but I did it. I experienced many more so called "break downs" during the following two years. I realized that every time I stood back up, another strong piece of me fell into place.

So how did the story end? After two years in court I could no longer afford the legal fees and court costs, and accepted their out of court settlement. In the end I lost a substantial amount of money.

So what did I learn from this experience? Well it reinforced in my heart, how wonderful my husband and kids were. They were my rock. It taught me that even though I was broke and on the verge of losing my home, that I was, in actuality, wealthy! I had my family, and we had each other and we all had our health. Just that alone is priceless! It taught me that even though situations in life might cause me to break, I will never be broken.

Today I thank God for everything that happened. I didn't know it at the time because I couldn't see the "big picture" but now know, that it was for the best. If I had not experienced that pain, I would have never done all the soul searching that now let's me live my best life. I have put my life in perspective. I now know what is important and what is not. I now know who is important, who is not, and I don't waste time on negative or mean spirited people. I am able to find joy and happiness with the people I love, doing even the simplest of things. I love my life and the people in it!

EXERCISE

1. Are you going through hard times right now in your life and you don't know how you are going to get through it? Try to look for the blessings in the situation.

2. Can you have faith and know there is a bigger picture that maybe you are not seeing right now. Maybe you are on this path to learn a life lesson that one day you will be thankful for!

Chapter Seventeen

BE CAREFUL WHAT YOU WISH FOR

I HAD A client who was a stay at home mom, married with two kids. She suspected that her husband was cheating on her. She prayed to God to give her a sign. That same day she came home early and found her husband in their bed with another woman.

Needless to say they broke up. Having been a stay at home mom for over twelve years, she knew she had to go back to work and their lives were going to dramatically change.

She eventually found a job but only working twenty hours a week which wasn't enough. She found it very painful to not be able to buy her kids school supplies, clothes, or to even bring them for an outing.

The next time I saw her she had this beat down tired energy. She explained that there had been major changes at her workplace. They had fired her immediate boss, gave her the position and had hired an assistant to now help her out. What a turnaround! She was now working full time.

She told me "I'm very grateful for all the wonderful things happening with my job, but it's all the other life challenges that pop up on a day to day basis, that is exhausting me" She went on to tell me that her husband was now showing up, offering to take her on vacation, and to buy her a car. He would ease her financial burdens, but only if she took him back. She knew she could never forgive him, so getting back together wasn't an option, but the constant strain of saying "no" was wearing her down. She was also having issues with her parents. She said "I don't understand why there are so many situations in my life where I feel I need to stay strong and choose what is right, it's exhausting me! I say my prayers and affirmations every day and I'm still faced with these challenges."

I myself was perplexed; this woman had become so strong in the last year. She was giving and loving. What was drawing in these situations of turmoil? "What are your prayers every morning?" I asked. "Every morning I ask God for courage and strength" she said.

It all made sense to me now. I went on to explain to her that when you affirm or wish for courage and strength God doesn't just *give* you courage and strength, he *gives you situations where you will need courage and strength*. Those prayers might have served her well when she didn't have the strength to get out of bed in the morning or the courage to get a job and raise her kids. She was one of the strongest people I know, it was time to ask for something different. "What exactly do you want in your life at this point" I asked. "I just wish to have peace and serenity" she replied. "Well then wish for peace and serenity!"

EXERCISE

1. Are there prayers or affirmations that you are currently using that might be bringing more of what you don't want in your life?

2. Write a prayer or affirmation that enriches your life which you can say each morning before you start your day.

Chapter Eighteen

BAH HUMBUG

ARE THERE ASPECTS of your life you are unhappy with? Perhaps you are feeling dissatisfied about your health, your weight, your relationships, or your job? Areas you know you need to change but haven't been able to bring yourself to change them.

We have all been there. Maybe you are caught up in the daily grind of life, maybe you feel you don't have the energy to change it or even the skills to turn things around. Let me share with you a tool that has helped me.

Are you familiar with the Charles Dickins novel A Christmas Carol? Well for those of you who are not, let me explain. At the beginning of the novel the main character Ebenezer Scrooge, is a cold hearted, tight fisted miser, who hated Christmas. Whenever he would see people enjoying Christmas or experiencing joy, he would crankily say "Bah, humbug". The night before Christmas, Scrooge is visited by the ghosts of Christmas past, present, and future. They take him on a journey showing him why he is the way he is. The ghosts show him that people who don't have enough money can still find happiness. The ghost of the future brings him to the future where people are celebrating his death, and his legacy is a cheap tombstone in an unkempt graveyard. He awakens to find it is Christmas morning and therefore not too late to change his ways. Scrooge goes on to live a life of joy, happiness and generosity, thanking his ghosts of Christmas for showing him what would happen if he didn't change. So just like Scrooge you can turn it around, before it is too late.

EXERCISE

1. Sit down in a quiet place where you can be alone and won't be disturbed. Take out a pen and paper and get ready to write. Keep in mind that no one will ever read what you are writing so be brutally honest. Write down the problem or the area which you would like to change or improve. Then write down what you are not happy about in that situation. How does that make you feel? Now if you don't do something about the situation, where will you be in six months, a year, five years, or even twenty years? Write it down in detail, so that the pain that the future holds by not changing becomes a reality in your mind. Feel it, cry over it, and then write some more. Write in detail. Maybe write a whole scenario of what an entire day would be like, if you didn't change. Envision yourself alone

with no partner by your side because you didn't invest time in your relationship and grew apart. Perhaps you are not present to witness your children grow up due to lung cancer, because you just couldn't commit to quit smoking. Make it a reality; make it YOUR reality if you don't change.

2. Now take another piece of paper and write all the benefits you will have if you do change the problem or situation. Do the same processes but this time, when you fast forward to the future, feel the wonderful emotions, think of the great life you can have if you do change. Again write in detail all the wonderful things that all the changes will bring.

3. You should now be able to break through the barriers that were preventing you from making these changes before. Suddenly where once you thought you didn't have the energy, you now do. Where once you thought you didn't know how to fix it, answers present themselves. If not go back and do it

again, you didn't open yourself up enough to the exercise and FEEL the emotions. Don't worry, with some practice you will get it!

So like Scrooge learned, with the right motivation you can change. In the future when you are faced with an area of your life that you know you need to do something about, just say "Bah, humbug," as you go lock yourself in your room knowing you will be visited by the ghost of the future.

Chapter Nineteen

MEDITATION

MEDITATION HAS BECOME the "word du jour," but do thoughts of meditation have you picturing yourself, sitting crossed legged thumb to index finger, saying "ahhhh", for hours on end, until your tailbone screams in agony? If so let me simplify it.

Meditation is widely known to reduce the effects of stress, boost the immune system, increase creativity and calm the mind. I could get into the four brain wave states and give a long winded explanation of how it works, but I won't. So here goes;

The right side of the brain is the scientific, logical side, and the left side of the brain is the creative, intuitive, and insightful side. Meditation balances these two sides of the brain, which allows the human mind to go beyond the thinking process into a state of awareness, and intuitiveness.

So now that we understand meditation a bit more and some of the benefits, next step is to try it. All you need is a set of ear plugs and then follow these simple steps.

Step one

Find a nice quiet place where you won't be disturbed for about 10 minutes (I go to my room, sit up in bed with my big fluffy pillows supporting my back). Get comfortable.

Step two

Insert ear plugs

Step three

Close your eyes and breath, slow inhale and slow exhale.
Eureka you've got it!

Now focus on your breath, and for beginners here is where the earplugs help. By blocking your ears it really magnifies the sound of your breathing. If you notice thoughts in your head, put them aside and refocus on your breathing.

When you first practice meditation sometimes the voice in your head will get very hyper and refuse to be quiet, like a disobedient child in the throes of a tantrum. If this happens just as you draw in your breath, say "inhale" in your mind and say "exhale" as you expel your breath. Once your mind resigns itself to the fact that you are not going to listen to the incessant chatter, it will eventually quieten down and you will be able to just concentrate on your breathing and relax.

The more you practice meditation, the quicker you go into that relaxed state. You will also notice that the more you meditate, the clearer your mind will be. Answers to questions you have been asking yourself will suddenly pop into your head. What is your life purpose? Should you take that new job? Do you join in that new business venture? These are all questions that once you have silenced your conscious mind; your subconscious mind will work on solving, and often provide the answers!

EXERCISE

1. Practice meditating for ten minutes every day.

Chapter Twenty

NEGATIVE ENERGY-
CLOAK YOURSELF

EVER SINCE I clawed out of the black hole that I was in after my business failed, and found my inner peace and tranquility, I avoid negativity like the plague. I surround myself only with positive people, and I now run from a negative person, like a rat scurrying from a sinking ship.

In my personal life, avoiding negative people is easy. I just surround myself with warm loving people. There are times however when I simply can't control who will be around or their conversations, (like dealing with clients, co-workers, or people in social settings.) To deal with this, I close my eyes and visualize myself wrapping a heavy dark blue velvet cloak around my shoulders. This cloak repels all negative conversations and their energy. I can be present and listen, but as long as I don't add to the negativity, then it doesn't affect me or lower my own energy. If you work in an environment where moral is down and people are constantly complaining, visualize every morning before you leave putting on your layer of protection. It has become so real to me I will often find my hands reaching to pull the cloak tighter around my body like a warm blanket as I'm sitting there listening to the people converse around me. The more that the people around me complain, and talk about the miseries of life; I use that time to silently thank the powers that be, for all the wonderful blessings in my life.

EXERCISE

1. Visualize a way to repel negativity in your life. The cloak works for me but use your imagination to find something that works for you.

2. The next time you know you will be faced with a situation where you know there will be negative people around, practice your technique that you developed to repel the negative energy.

Chapter Twenty One

LIVE THE LIFE OF YOUR DREAMS

How YOU LIVE your daily life determines your future. If you want to live an awesome life, live an awesome day! You are the creator of your life. Imagine yourself a sculptor, and carve out the life of your dreams!

To live the life of your dreams, you need to know what those dreams are. Have you mapped out the journey that is your life? Chances are you have never taken the time to think about what you would like to do, have, or be. You have never taken the time to dream or set goals.

You wouldn't leave on vacation and just get in your car without any destination in mind, would you? No. You would decide what you want to do, where you want to go, what you would like to experience, before having left. Often we spend more time planning and mapping out our vacations than our own lives!

While although I believe "life is a journey, not a destination," this doesn't mean the destination isn't important. You can have both! A wonderful journey full of joy and happiness AND a wonderful destination! You just need a map to guide you along the way, and this map is your life goals.

You need to become clear on what you want, in all the areas of your life! Can't think of what you want? Then think of what you don't want, and simply reverse it. Goal setting is one of the most important things you could ever do for yourself and your life. Knowing what you want out of life is a powerful way of mapping your future!

EXERCISE

1. Set some goals. Decide what you want to do with your life. Think of what you would like to have in all major areas. Personal, family, career, financial, health and pleasure.

2. State each goal like it has already happened and use motivational language. For example "I absolutely love my new home overlooking the ocean."

3. Review your goals daily as you envision what your life would be like if you had already achieved them.

4. As you reach your goals and gain confidence, set new goals—dream big—the possibilities are endless!

BIOGRAPHY

For over two decades, T.C. Downing has helped countless people find their inner and outer beauty. An avid reader and researcher in the domain of personal development and well-being, have resulted in helping many people live their best lives. She currently resides with her husband and two children in Montreal, Canada.

Made in the USA
Las Vegas, NV
15 April 2022

47518023R00073